Learn Catalan with Parlem tu i jo

HypLern Interlinear Project
www.hyplern.com

First edition: 2025, September

Author: Rafael Vallbona
Translation: Michael Nock
Foreword: Camilo Andrés Bonilla Carvajal PhD

ISBN: 1989643159

kees@hyplern.com
www.hyplern.com

Learn Catalan with Parlem tu i jo

Interlinear Catalan to English

Author
Rafael Vallbona

Translation
Michael Nock

HypLern Interlinear Project
www.hyplern.com

The HypLern Method

Learning a foreign language should not mean leafing through page after page in a bilingual dictionary until one's fingertips begin to hurt. Quite the contrary, through everyday language use, friendly reading, and direct exposure to the language we can get well on our way towards mastery of the vocabulary and grammar needed to read native texts. In this manner, learners can be successful in the foreign language without too much study of grammar paradigms or rules. Indeed, Seneca expresses in his sixth epistle that "Longum iter est per praecepta, breve et efficax per exempla[1]."

The HypLern series constitutes an effort to provide a highly effective tool for experiential foreign language learning. Those who are genuinely interested in utilizing original literary works to learn a foreign language do not have to use conventional graded texts or adapted versions for novice readers. The former only distort the actual essence of literary works, while the latter are highly reduced in vocabulary and relevant content. This collection aims to bring the lively experience of reading stories as directly told by their very authors to foreign language learners.

Most excited adult language learners will at some point seek their teachers' guidance on the process of learning to read in the foreign language rather than seeking out external opinions. However, both teachers and learners lack a general reading technique or strategy. Oftentimes, students undertake the reading task equipped with nothing more than a bilingual dictionary, a grammar book, and lots of courage. These efforts often end in frustration as the student builds mis-constructed nonsensical sentences after many hours spent on an aimless translation drill.

Consequently, we have decided to develop this series of interlinear translations intended to afford a comprehensive edition of unabridged texts. These texts are presented as they were originally written with no changes in word choice or order. As a result, we have a translated piece conveying the true meaning under every word from the original work. Our readers receive then two books in just one volume: the original version and its translation.

The reading task is no longer a laborious exercise of patiently decoding unclear and seemingly complex paragraphs. What's more, reading becomes an enjoyable and meaningful process of cultural, philosophical and linguistic learning. Independent learners can then acquire expressions and vocabulary while understanding pragmatic and socio-cultural dimensions of the target language by reading in it rather than reading about it.

Our proposal, however, does not claim to be a novelty. Interlinear translation is as old as the Spanish tongue, e.g. "glosses of [Saint] Emilianus", interlinear bibles in Old German, and of course James Hamilton's work in the 1800s. About the latter, we remind the readers, that as a revolutionary freethinker he promoted the publication of Greco-Roman classic works and further pieces in diverse languages. His effort, such as ours, sought to lighten the exhausting task of looking words up in large glossaries as an educational practice: "if there is any thing which fills reflecting men with melancholy and regret, it is the waste of mortal time, parental money, and puerile happiness, in the present method of pursuing Latin and Greek[2]".

Additionally, another influential figure in the same line of thought as Hamilton was John Locke. Locke was also the philosopher and translator of the Fabulae AEsopi in an interlinear plan. In 1600, he was already suggesting that interlinear texts, everyday communication, and use of the target language could be the most appropriate ways to achieve language learning:

> ...the true and genuine Way, and that which I would propose, not only as the easiest and best, wherein a Child might, without pains or Chiding, get a Language which others are wont to be whipt for at School six or seven Years together...[3]

---

1 "The journey is long through precepts, but brief and effective through examples". Seneca, Lucius Annaeus. (1961) Ad Lucilium Epistulae Morales, vol. I. London: W. Heinemann.

2 In: Hamilton, James (1829?) History, principles, practice and results of the Hamiltonian system, with answers to the Edinburgh and Westminster reviews; A lecture delivered at Liverpool; and instructions for the use of the books published on the system. Londres: W. Aylott and Co., 8, Pater Noster Row. p. 29.

3 In: Locke, John. (1693) Some thoughts concerning education. Londres: A. and J. Churchill. pp. 196-7.

Who can benefit from this edition?

We identify three kinds of readers, namely, those who take this work as a search tool, those who want to learn a language by reading authentic materials, and those attempting to read writers in their original language. The HypLern collection constitutes a very effective instrument for all of them.

1. For the first target audience, this edition represents a search tool to connect their mother tongue with that of the writer's. Therefore, they have the opportunity to read over an original literary work in an enriching and certain manner.
2. For the second group, reading every word or idiomatic expression in its actual context of use will yield a strong association between the form, the collocation, and the context. This will have a direct impact on long term learning of passive vocabulary, gradually building genuine reading ability in the original language. This book is an ideal companion not only to independent learners but also to those who take lessons with a teacher. At the same time, the continuous feeling of achievement produced during the process of reading original authors both stimulates and empowers the learner to study[1].
3. Finally, the third kind of reader will notice the same benefits as the previous ones. The proximity of a word and its translation in our interlinear texts is a step further from other collections, such as the Loeb Classical Library. Although their works might be considered the most famous in this genre, the presentation of texts on opposite pages hinders the immediate link between words and their semantic equivalence in our native tongue (or one we have a strong mastery of).

---

1 Some further ways of using the present work include:

1. As you progress through the stories, focus less on the lower line (the English translation). Instead, try to read through the upper line, staying in the foreign language as long as possible.
2. Even if you find glosses or explanatory footnotes about the mechanics of the language, you should make your own hypotheses on word formation and syntactical functions in a sentence. Feel confident about inferring your own language rules and test them progressively. You can also take notes concerning those idiomatic expressions or special language usage that calls your attention for later study.
3. As soon as you finish each text, check the reading in the original version (with no interlinear or parallel translation). This will fulfil the main goal of this

collection: bridging the gap between readers and original literary works, training them to read directly and independently.

Why interlinear?

Conventionally speaking, tiresome reading in tricky and exhausting circumstances has been the common definition of learning by texts. This collection offers a friendly reading format where the language is not a stumbling block anymore. Contrastively, our collection presents a language as a vehicle through which readers can attain and understand their authors' written ideas.

While learning to read, most people are urged to use the dictionary and distinguish words from multiple entries. We help readers skip this step by providing the proper translation based on the surrounding context. In so doing, readers have the chance to invest energy and time in understanding the text and learning vocabulary; they read quickly and easily like a skilled horseman cantering through a book.

Thereby we stress the fact that our proposal is not new at all. Others have tried the same before, coming up with evident and substantial outcomes. Certainly, we are not pioneers in designing interlinear texts. Nonetheless, we are nowadays the only, and doubtless, the best, in providing you with interlinear foreign language texts.

Handling instructions

Using this book is very easy. Each text should be read at least three times in order to explore the whole potential of the method. The first phase is devoted to comparing words in the foreign language to those in the mother tongue. This is to say, the upper line is contrasted to the lower line as the following example shows:

Les	cases	perdudes	de	Rafael	Vallbona
The	houses	lost	by	Rafael	Vallbona

The second phase of reading focuses on capturing the meaning and sense of the original text. As readers gain practice with the method, they should be able to focus on the target language without getting distracted by the translation. New users of the method, however, may find it helpful to cover the translated lines with a piece of paper as illustrated in the image below. Subsequently, they try to understand the meaning of every word, phrase, and entire sentences in the target language itself, drawing on the translation only when necessary. In this phase, the reader should resist the temptation to look at the translation for every word. In doing so, they will find that they are able to understand a good portion of the text by reading directly in the target language, without the crutch of the translation. This is the skill we are looking to train: the ability to read and understand native materials and enjoy them as native speakers do, that being, directly in the original language.

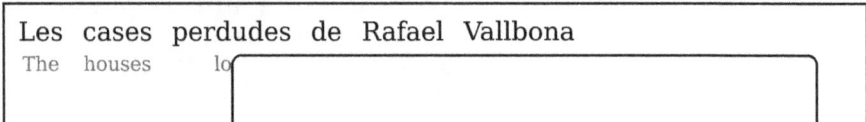

Les cases perdudes de Rafael Vallbona
The houses lo

In the final phase, readers will be able to understand the meaning of the text when reading it without additional help. There may be some less common words and phrases which have not cemented themselves yet in the reader's brain, but the majority of the story should not pose any problems. If desired, the reader can use an SRS or some other memorization method to learning these straggling words.

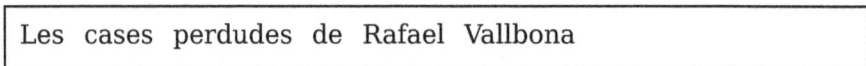

Les cases perdudes de Rafael Vallbona

Above all, readers will not have to look every word up in a dictionary to read a text in the foreign language. This otherwise wasted time will be spent concentrating on their principal interest. These new readers will tackle authentic texts while learning their vocabulary and expressions to use in further communicative (written or oral) situations. This book is just one work from an overall series with the same purpose. It really helps those who are afraid of having "poor vocabulary" to feel confident about reading directly in the language. To all of them and to all of you, welcome to the amazing experience of living a foreign language!

Additional tools

Check out shop.hyplern.com or contact us at info@hyplern.com for free mp3s (if available) and free empty (untranslated) versions of the eBooks that we have on offer.

For some of the older eBooks and paperbacks we have Windows, iOS and Android apps available that, next to the interlinear format, allow for a pop-up format, where hovering over a word or clicking on it gives you its meaning. The apps also have any mp3s, if available, and integrated vocabulary practice.

Visit the site hyplern.com for the same functionality online. This is where we will be working non-stop to make all our material available in multiple formats, including audio where available, and vocabulary practice.

Table of Contents

Chapter	Page
1 - Les cases perdudes	1
2 - Mens sana in corpore quiet	21
3 - Déu i el senyor Gratacòs	41
4 - Vuit setmanes i tres dies	65

Les cases perdudes
The houses lost (The lost houses)

Les cases perdudes de Rafael Vallbona
The houses lost by Rafael Vallbona

Planta baixa: mai no he dubtat que la casa ens
Floor low never not have I doubted that the house us
The ground floor never have I

  tria, i a això hi destinem els esforços de
chooses and to that to it we allocate the efforts of

part de la vida. L'experiència dels humans és
part of the life The experience of -the- humans is
    our

diferent; no tant pel que som, com pel que
different not so much for the that we are as for the that
    for what for what

volem ser. Les cases on habitem
we want to be The houses where we live

  al llarg dels anys són una de les percepcions
to the length of the years are one of the perceptions
  throughout the

més íntimament lligades al pas del temps
most intimately tied to the passing of -the- time

i la mortalitat, les grans pors que mouen la
and -the- mortality the great fears that move -the-

vida. Així, una casa lluminosa, càlida a l'hivern i
life So a house bright / well-lit warm in the winter and

fresca a l'estiu, i prou espaiosa per a les
fresh in the summer and enough spacious for to / for -the-

nostres necessitats, ens concedeix una vida digna.
our necessities us concedes / offers a life honorable

Decència i honestedat són dues forces
Decency and honesty are two forces

imprescindibles per superar la por a descobrir
indispensable for overcoming the fear to / of discovering

la realitat que ens fa ser com som.
the reality that us makes / makes us be be as we are

De petit vivia amb els pares i els avis
From small / as a child I lived with the / my parents and the / my grandparents

paterns en un pis fosc i fred, de llarg
paternal in an apartment dark and cold with / with a long

3

passadís, cambres mal ventilades, sostres alts, i
corridor rooms badly ventilated roofs high and

massa silencis que mai no se'm va permetre
too much silence that never not one to me did allow
was I allowed

trencar. Una àvia totpoderosa marcava el
to break A grandmother all-powerful marked the

ritme gris del dia a dia, que només la ferrenya
rhythm gray of the day to day that only the strong

voluntat del seu marit, impedit de parlar
willpower of -the- her husband impeded from speaking

per una embòlia, gosava qüestionar.
by an embolism dared to question
because of blood clot

L'aquiescència impotent del fill i una
The acquiescence impotent of the son and a

progressiva amargor de la jove, donaven a
progressive bitterness of the young woman gave to

l'habitatge un perfil llòbrec i dolorós que jo
the dwelling a profile gloomy and painful that I

només   trencava   submergint-me
only   broke   submersing-myself

una i altra vegada en la lectura de la
one and another time   in the reading of the
          time after time

col·lecció de les aventures d'en Massagran, un dels
collection of the adventures of   Massagran   one of the

pocs libres per a nens que hi havia a
few   books   for to children that there was   in
           for

l'aparador de portes de vidre que presidia la
the display case with doors of glass that presided the
          glass doors

sala, en realitat un eixamplament del passadís
living room in reality a   widening   of the corridor

presidit per dues butaques   d'hule   i un
presided by two armchairs (made) of oilskin and an

enorme telèfon negre de baquelita que   feia
enormous telephone black of Bakellite that made (one)

saltar d'esglai quan sonava.
jump from fright when it sounded
          rang

5

Aquell no era l'hàbitat més propici per ser feliç
That not was the habitat most favorable to be happy

amb la intensitat amb què un nen és capaç,
with the intensity with which a boy is capable

encara que els adults opinin el contrari, o sigui
still that the adults think the opposite or is
even if   in other words

que vaig fer mans i mànigues per demanar una
that I did make hands and sleeves to ask for a
          I did everything possible and more

mena d'acolliment temporal a casa dels altres
sort of shelter temporary at home of the other
                                                                    of my

avis. Era un pis petit, bigarrat i
grandparents It was an apartment small all jumbled and

ofegat de llum des de primera hora, amb el
suffocated of light from the first hour with the
          by   from   early in the morning

brogit del mercat de l'Abaceria Central, que era
sound of the market of the Abaceria Central which was
                              grocery store

a tocar de casa que desvetllava un dormilega
at touch of house which would wake up a sleepyhead
very close to our house

i un intens aroma de cafè torrat que embafava
and an intense aroma of coffee roasted which satiated

agradablement la pituïtària. Els discos
pleasantly the pituitary The discs
pituitary gland

dels Sírex de la tieta, les bromes
of the Sírex of the auntie the jokes
{a Spanish rock band} my

escatològiques de l'avi i la passió per la
scatological of the grandpa and the passion for -the-
about poop my grandpa

seva Ramona, marcaven un dia a dia esbojarrat
her Ramona marked a day to day crazy

del matí a la nit. En aquella casa les
from the morning to the night In that house the

normes de comportament eren tan franques i
rules of behavior were as clear and

relaxades com el desordre que hi havia per
relaxed as the disorder that there was for
throughout

tot el pis.
all the apartment
the whole

Aquella va ser una època d'una profunda
That did be a time of a profound
      was

conformació del meu caràcter; prou que ho
structuring of -the- my character enough that it
      certainly

veig ara per comparació.
I see now for comparison
    in

Principal: la casa d'adolescència sol ser un
Most important the house of (one's) adolescence tends to be a
Main apartment

avorriment del qual ens n'oblidem
boredom about -the- which ourselves of it we forget
      we forget about it

així que ens fem una mica grans, per
such that ourselves we make a little old for
as soon as   we get   older

conforts i privilegis que ens pugui donar la
comforts and privileges that us can give the
      our

família. Cansats d'acumular fel i assentiments,
family Tired of accumulating bile and approvals

els pares van llogar un pis en un poble del
the parents did rent an apartment in a village of the
my   rented

litoral. L'únic bon record no inventat d'aquella
coast the only good memory not invented from that

època és l'agradable sensació de sentir-me
time is the pleasant sensation of feeling myself
                                                    feeling

a tocar del mar durant tot el trajecte en el
at touch of the sea during all the trip in the
close to the   the entire

600 del pare, de la ciutat grisa i vençuda
(SEAT) 600 of the father of the city gray and conquered
{type of car} of my

a aquella nova expectativa emocional. La intensitat
by that new expectation emotional The intensity

de la blavor d'aquella aigua m'ha quedat
of the blue of that water me has stayed
                                          has been

per sempre gravada a la carta de colors de la
for always engraved in the menu of colors of the
    forever

memòria.
memory

El pis era gran i de llum no estava
The apartment was big and of light not it was
                          with regard to   it wasn't

malament. Els carrers d'aquell eixample
bad the streets of that suburban development

nou per a immigrants conferien un territori
new for to immigrants conferred a territory
for

d'aventura raonable per a algú que creixia amb
of adventure reasonable for to someone who grew with
for

ales a les sabates. Tot i que l'havia de
wings in the shoes All and that it I had to
their even though

compartir amb el meu germà, l'habitació era
share with -the- my brother the room was

prou espaiosa per a un modest embrió de
enough spacious for to a modest embryo of
spacious enough for

biblioteca personal, la cuina feia olor de nou i
library personal the kitchen made smell of new and
smelled like

el fred era suportable. El poble tenia un aire
the cold was bearable The village had an air

feréstec que mai no havia tastat. Tot semblaven
wild that never not I had tasted All seemed like
I had never They all

avantatges.
advantages

Però l'adolescència és temps de revoltes, de
But -the- adolescence is time of revolt of
a time

destruir tot allò que s'ha aixecat i buscar
destroying all that that itself has lifted and looking for
everything has risen

nous camins a l'existència radicalment diferents
new paths to -the- existence radically different

als solcats fins llavors. La casa
from the plowed up until then The house
ones walked

ens cau al damunt, el paper pseudopop de les
us falls to the above the paper pseudopop of the
falls on top of us

parets és la imatge del monstre generacional que
walls is the image of the monster generational that

amaguem amb pòsters de mites fugissers, i la
we hide with posters of myths fleeting and the

nova personalitat busca experiències vitals tan
new personality looks for experiences vital as

precàries com l'existència. No hi ha més raons.
precarious as the existence Not there is more reasons
                                         there aren't any more

Primer pis: amb un col·lega vaig llogar una
First floor with a pal I did rent a
                                    I rented

habitació del pis d'uns amics
room of the apartment of some friends

amb vistes al celobert. Era una estança trista,
with views to the inner patio It was an abode sad
with a view of the

de parets tacades d'humitat, un tuf permanent
with walls stained with humidity a stench permanent

barreja de resclosit i bròquil bullit que pujava
mix of stuffiness and broccoli boiled which rose

pel pati eufemísticament dit de llums, una
through the patio euphemistically said of lights a

bombeta pelada al sostre que tenyia
light bulb bare in the ceiling that dyed

d'un groc tísic l'espai, i un
with a yellow consumptive the space and a
with a consumptive yellow

armari encastat tan ple de llibres, diaris vells
wardrobe embedded as full of books newspapers old
fitted wardrobe

i inclassificables records d'amors nonats, com de
and inclassifiable memories of loves unborn as of

fongs i pols.
fungi and dust

Com no és difícil d'imaginar en un habitatge de
As not it is difficult to imagine in a dwelling of

joves, la cuina era un santuari de la
young people the kitchen was a sanctuary of -the-

microbiologia gràcies als protozous ciliats,
microbiology thanks to the protozoa ciliated

nascuts de la putrefacció de menjucs d'origen
born from the putrefaction of snacks of origin

qüestionable però destí clar: els plats bruts
questionable but destination clear the plates dirty

entollats dins l'aigüera uns quants dies. Del
swamped in the sink a few days Of the
piled up

13

lavabo n'estalvio la descripció per no
bathroom of it I save the description in order to not
  I'll leave out its description

provocar més nàusees entre els amables lectors.
provoke more nauseas among the kind readers

Ara bé, la sala d'estar era el més similar
now well the room of being was the most similar
having said that living room

al paradís que mai no havia conegut: al
to -the- paradise that never not I had known in the
  I had ever

portentós estèreo hi sonava tot el dia els
marvelous stereo there sounded all the day the

Stones, Lou Reed o Led Zeppelin; mentre que,
Stones Lou Reed or Led Zeppelin while that
  whereas

del crepuscle a l'albada, l'espai estava envaït
from -the- twighlight to -the- dawn the space was invaded

per la subtilesa de Pink Floyd, Miles Davis o
by the subtlety of Pink Floyd Miles Davis or

Leonard Cohen si ens sentíem lírics. La tènue
Leonard Cohen if ourselves we felt lyrical The faint
  we were feeling

llum d'espelmes, l'olor penetrant del sàndal
light of candles the smell penetrating of the sandalwood
   candlelight

i una immensa moqueta pàtria d'àcars,
and an immense wall-to-wall carpet homeland to mites

contribuïen a fer volar les nostres quimeres
contributed to making fly -the- our fantasies
       blowing up

lluny de la grisor del temps i la
far away from the grayness of -the- time and the

desolació del pis.
desolation of the apartment

Tot l'apartament era un lloc lamentable, però la
All the apartment was a place pitiful but the
the entire apartment

imaginació s'enduia el cos allà on jo volia, i
imagination took itself the body there where I wanted and
    took one's body

va ser en aquest territori tan contrari al
it did be in this territory as contrary to -the-
it was

sentit comú com cert en el meu imaginari,
sense common as certain in -the- my imaginary (one)

que vaig fer el primer pas per a superar la por
that I did make the first step for to overcome the fear
   I took   to

a l'existència i vaig decidir que intentaria bastir
of -the- existence and I did decide that I would build

la meva experiència humana essent escriptor.
-the- my experience human being (a) writer

Àtic: la veritat és ficció i les cases on vivim
Attic the truth is fiction and the houses where we live

la seva construcció. El sentit final de
-the- their construction The meaning final of

l'existència consisteix a saber que tot és
-the- existence consists of knowing that all is

imaginat i, bo i sabent-ho, habitar en ella.
imagined and good and knowing it living in it

Així sobrevivim al pas del temps i
That's how we survive -to- the pass of -the- time and

al to misèrrim de la condició humana.
-to- the tone extremely miserable of the condition human

Visc en una casa de poble. El meu estudi,
I live in a house of village -The- my study
village house

al pis de dalt, és un espai obert al mar i
in the floor of above is a space open to the sea and
upstairs

al verd que encatifa la serralada, embotit de
to the green that carpets the mountain range packed with

llibres i quadres, i amb la confortabilitat
books and paintings and with the comfortability

per a treballar-hi que sempre havia desitjat. Aquí
for to work there that always I had wished for Here
to

escric i fent-ho he pagat la hipoteca. Ja
I write and doing it I have paid the mortgage Already

sé que hi ha molta gent que pensa que
I know that there are many people that think that

escrivint no es poden pagar les factures, però
writing not one can pay the bills but
by writing

jo ho faig de fa molts anys.
I it do since ago many years
I have done it many years ago

De la cuina en puja una aroma de rostit
From the kitchen -from it- rises an aroma of roast

amb prunes i pinyons que atia els sentits
with plums and pine nuts that rouses the senses

capritxosament, mentre la ment pensa en el
capriciously while the mind thinks in/about the

merlot que l'acompanyarà; a fora sé que a
merlot that will accompany it -at- outside I know that in

l'estiu m'espera, impol·luta com el mirall que
the summer awaits me unpolluted/pure as the mirror that

sempre ens enganya, la piscina, i a la
always us deceives the pool and in the

sala d'estar un modern equip de música em
room of being / living room a modern equipment of music / stereo me

transporta als paisatges més calms de l'ànima
transports to the landscapes most calm / calmest of the soul

a través del piano de Keith Jarrett, bo i
to through / through the of the piano of Keith Jarret good and

escarxofat en un còmode sofà de pell. Els
sprawled out on a comfortable sofa (made) of leather The
My

amics beuen un bon whisky o un brandi quan a
friends drink a good whisky or a brandy when in

l'hivern encenem la llar de foc, el vestidor
the winter light the hearth of fire the dressing room
fireplace

conté el nombre necessari de camises i vestits,
contains the number necessary of shirts and suits
amount

i un cotxe suficient m'espera al garatge
and a car sufficient awaits me in the garage
decent enough

per si vull desarrelar-me temporalment.
for if I want to uproot myself temporarily
in case

Cremades totes les cambres, a la vida adulta
Burned all the rooms in the life adult
all of

no hi ha més compassió que aquesta. Perduda
not there is more compassion than this one Lost
there is no other

la innocència, els anys i els tràngols
the innocence the years and the difficult situations
our

ensenyen que totes les cases del nostre
show *that* *all (of)* *the* *houses* *of -the-* *our*

deambular són caselles del joc de la vida. I
wandering *are* *squares* *of the* *game* *of* *-the-* *life* *And*

com a personatges d'aquesta representació, cal
as *to* *characters* *of this* *representation* *one must*

transitar-les.
travel them

Mens sana in corpore quiet

Mind sane in body quiet (A sane mind in a quiet body)

De sobte, la negror de l'habitació es va
Of sudden the blackness of the room itself did
suddenly darkness

il·luminar amb les coloraines d'uns números i
illuminate with the bright colors of some numbers and

una data. El rellotge despertador havia piulat a
a date The clock alarm had chirped at

l'hora programada. Set del matí, vuit de
the time programmed Seven of the morning eight(h) of
in the

gener, 2053. L'home va obrir els ulls i, sense
January 2053 The man did open the eyes and without
opened his

moure's encara del llit, va engrapar el
moving -himself- still in the bed did grab the

mòbil de la tauleta i va teclejar unes
cellphone from the little table and did type some

ordres. Primera ordre: climatitzar la casa
commands First order to air condition the house

perquè, en llevar-se, la seva dona i
so that upon getting -himself- up -the- his wife and

el seu fill trobessin l'escalfor que es
-the- his son (they) would find the warmth that -themselves-

mereixien. Segona ordre: activar la cafetera
(they) deserved second order to activate the coffee maker

i el microones de la cuina perquè, una vegada
and the microwave of the kitchen so that a time
once

dutxat i vestit, ell pogués assaborir l'esmorzar
showered and dressed he could savor the breakfast

que també es mereixia. Tercera ordre:
that also -himself- (he) deserved Third order

engegar el cotxe a distància, fer-lo maniobrar tot
turn on the car at distance make it maneuver all
remotely

sol fora del garatge i deixar-lo aparcat amb
alone out of the garage and leave it parked with
by itself

pulcritud   davant   la   porta mateixa   de   la   casa
neatness   in front of   the   door   same   of   the   house
the very door

perquè   ella   el   tingués   a   punt   trenta   minuts
so that   she   it   had   at   point   thirty   minutes
ready

després,   quan   anés   a   treballar   a   l'oficina.
after   when   (she) went   to   work   at   the office

Encara   en   pijama,   va   sortir   de   l'habitació
Still   in   pajamas   (he) did   leave   from   the room

sense   fer   fressa   i   va   anar   a   ullar   l'habitació
without   making   noise   and   did   go   to   eye   the room
check out

del   nen.   L'Ernest   dormia   amb   la   placidesa
of the   boy   -The- Ernest   was sleeping   with   the   placidness

dels   qui   acaben   de   complir   set   anys.
of those   who   end up   of   complete(d)   seven   years (old)
have just   turned

Aleshores   va   canviar   d'idea.   En   comptes
Then   (he) did   change   of idea   In   stead
his mind

d'enfilar   cap   a   la   dutxa,   va   pujar   les
of heading   towards   -to-   the   shower   (he) did   ascend   the

escales i va entrar a l'estudi. Estirat a
steps and did enter to the study (Having) lain down at / on

terra encarat al sostre va dur-se les
(the) ground faced / facing to the ceiling (he) did bring himself the / his

mans al clatell i, després de dubtar-ho
hands to the nape of neck and after -of- hesitat(ing) -it-

una estona, va començar a flexionar el cos
a bit (he) did start to flex the body

endavant i endarrere, una mica esporuguit
forward and back a little frightened

perquè sabia que amb aquells moviments
because (he) knew that with those movements

corporals infringia la llei però alhora satisfet
of the body violated the law but at the same time satisfied

amb ell mateix perquè s'havia demostrat que
with he same because to himself he had demonstrated that

era capaç d'anar a contra corrent. Al cap
(he) was capable of going -to- against (the) current At the end / After

d'un quart d'hora el mòbil va avisar-lo que,
-of- a quarter of (an) hour the cellphone did notify him that

ara sí, calia despertar el seu fill per
now yes it was necessary to wake up -the- his son to

dur-lo a l'escola. Va obrir la porta i va
bring him to -the- school (He) did open the door and did

contemplar-lo en silenci un parell de minuts més.
contemplate him in silence a couple of minutes more

L'Ernest tenia un caminar de pardal. Mai havia
-The- Ernest had a walk of sparrow Never (he) had

corregut. Ni un sol salt, li havia vist fer.
run Not even a single jump him (he) had seen make

No li podia pas retreure, era un nano
Not him could not reproach (he) was a child

disciplinat, acostumat a seguir les normes
well-behaved accustomed to following the rules

establertes. Més o menys com tothom. O com
established More or less like everyone Or like

gairebé tothom perquè sempre n'hi ha d'agosarats
almost everyone because always there are some bold ones

disposats a desafiar les autoritats. És clar que
ready to challenge the authorities (It) is clear that

els agosarats que arrencaven a córrer enmig
the bold ones that started to run in the middle

del carrer o que improvisaven un partit de futbol
of the street or that improvised a match of soccer

en un descampat podien acabar en garjoles petites
in a clearing could end up in cells small

i humides, de poc més d'un metre perquè
and wet of little more than a meter so that

ni tan sols es poguessin moure. Aquest era
nor so only themselves (they) could move This was
not even

el càstig per als que feien saltirons i
the punishment for those that made hops and

flexions, dues paraules que fins i tot havien
push ups two words that until and all had
even

quedat proscrites del llenguatge ciutadà. Sovint,
stayed / been — prohibited — from the — language / everyday language — citizen — Often

les preguntes de l'Ernest li resultaven
the — questions — of — -the- Ernest — to him — (they) resulted / were

incòmodes.
uncomfortable

—Pare, els animals corren i salten. Per què no
Father — the — animals — run — and — jump — For what / Why — not

podem fer-ho, nosaltres?
(we) can — do it — ourselves

—Perquè està prohibit.
Because — (it) is — prohibited

—I per què, està prohibit?
And — for — what — is (it) — prohibited

—Perquè és dolent per a la salut.
Because — (it) is — bad — for — -to- — the — health

A vegades, per reconfortar-lo i perquè
At — times — to — comfort him — and — so that

agafés el son, s'arrupia al costat del
(he) would grasp the sleep himself huddles at the side of the
he would fall asleep squats

llit i li explicava històries del passat, quan
bed and to him (he) explained stories of the past when

els xandalls i les bambes encara es
the tracksuits and the sneakers still -themselves-

podien comprar.
(they) could (be) buy
bought

—Xandalls?
Tracksuits

—Sí, fill meu, roba expressa per a poder córrer
Yes son my clothes especially for to be able to run

amb més comoditat.
with more comfort

I l'Ernest obria un pam d'ulls escoltant
And -the- Ernest opened a span of eyes listening
{hand palm}

com li parlava d'un temps en què a l'hora
how to him (he) talked of a time in which at the time
during

del   pati   els nens i les nenes   podien
-of the- playground the boys and the   girls   (they) could
          recess

jugar   a   empaitar-se, quan fins i   tot existia
play   at   chase each other when until and all existed
      the game of   even

una assignatura que avaluava les seves qualitats
a   subject   that evaluated -the- their qualities
     class

gimnàstiques. Un temps en què ell encara tenia
gymnastics   A   time   in which he   still   had

un lloc de treball, fent de monitor al   gimnàs
a place of   work   making as a monitor at the   gym
                working

del barri.
of the neighborhood

—Gimnàs, pare?
  Gym   father

—Sí, fill meu. Un lloc   on   la gent   es
Yes son   my   a   place where the people -themselves-

podia divertir estiu i   hivern practicant el
could have fun summer and winter   practicing -the-

seu   esport preferit.
his/her   sport   preferred
                  favorite

Tot   va   començar   el   dia   que   l'Organització
(It) all   did   start   the   day   that   the Organization

Mundial   de   la   Salut   va   emetre   l'informe   que
Worldwide   of   -the-   Health   did   emit   the report   that

demostrava   els   efectes   perjudicials   que   la   pràctica
proved   the   effects   harmful   that   the   practice

de   l'esport   provocava   sobre   l'organisme   humà.
of   -the- sport   provoked   on   the organism   human

Després   van   venir   més   informes,   l'empenta   dels
After   did   come   more   reports   the push   of the

grups   fonamentalistes   i   finalment   la   miraculosa
groups   fundamentalists   and   finally   the   miraculous

píndola   que   permetia   obtenir   els   mateixos   efectes
pill   that   allowed   to get   the   very   effects

de   l'exercici   físic   sense   aixecar-se   de   la
of   the exercise   physical   without   to get up oneself   from   the

cadira. Ara els fonamentalistes eren al govern
chair Now the fundamentalists were in the government

i la píndola s'administrava massivament a
and the pill itself was administered massively to

una població addicta i manyaga. Camí de
a population addicted and docile (The) road of
On the way to

l'escola, l'Ernest es va embadocar amb un
the school -the- Ernest himself did to distract with a

estol d'estornells que dibuixava giragonses al cel,
flock of starlings that drew curves in the sky

ben a prop del campanar, lluitant contra la
well -to- near to the bell tower fighting against the
very

primera ventada de la tardor. El seu pare sabia
first wind of the autumn -The- his father knew

prou bé que envejava aquells ocells, els seus
enough well that (he) envied those birds -the- their

capgirells voladors, sobretot la seva llibertat de
"head-turns" flying above all -the- their freedom of
somersaults

moviments. Aleshores, en tombar la cantonada
movements   Then   upon turning the   corner

hi   van   topar.   Un   jove   baixava
there (they) did to bump into A young man was coming down

corrent, suat, cansat i amb cara d'espant perquè
running sweaty tired and with face of fear because

l'havien   enxampat corrent. El   pare   el   va
him (they) had caught   running The father him did

fitar   uns segons i va dir vinga, Ernest, anem,
to stare some seconds and did say come on Ernest (we) go
                                                   let's go

que   fem   tard. El noi ho va aprofitar   per
-that- (we) make late The boy it did take advantage to
       we are

allunyar-se   amb   passes   lentes,   capcot,
distance himself   with   steps   slow   head down
get away

tombant-se   de tant en tant   per comprovar
turning himself   of so much in so much to check
                  from time to time

que de debò havien decidit no delatar-lo.   Llavors
that of real (they) had decided not to tell on him Then
if   really

el pare va saber també que li acabava de
the father did know also that to him (he) had just -of-
realized

donar al seu fill la primera lliçó d'adult: la
to give to -the- his son the first lesson of adult -the-
given

gent com cal no delata ningú. Quan
people as is necessary not betray anyone When
decent people

l'Ernest va fer vuit anys, va decidir que
-the- Ernest did to make eight years (old) (he) did decide that
turned

li ensenyaria allò. Va agafar-lo de la mà
to him (he) would teach that (He) did grab him of the hand
by

i van anar plegats fins a un pis del
and (they) did go together until to an apartment of the
up to

barri vell que tenia una escala estreta i
neighborhood old that had a stairway narrow and

costeruda. Al capdamunt de l'escala, al
steep At the top of the stairway at the

darrer pis, els va obrir un home que devia
last apartment them did open a man that must have

tenir la mateixa edat del pare.
have   the   same   age   of the father
had   as the

—De veritat   vols   que   li   ho ensenyi?, —va
Of   truth (do you) want that to him it (I) teach   did
    Really

preguntar l'home. —Si la policia ho descobrís, em
ask   the man If the police it finds out   me

detindria a mi, però a vosaltres dos, també.
would arrest to me but -to- you   two   also

—Sí, vull que li ho ensenyis. Serà el seu
yes (I) want that to him it (you) teach Will be -it- his

regal d'aniversari.
gift -of- birthday

L'home va acompanyar-los a una sala desproveïda
The man did accompany them to a room   deprived

de mobles, amb un únic objecte tapat amb un
of furniture with a sole object covered with a

llençol. Amb un toc de solemnitat va
bed sheet With a touch of solemnity (he) did

35

arraconar   el llençol i l'Ernest va baixar la
put in the corner the bed sheet and -the- ernest did lower the
                                                              his

barbeta dos   dits,   meravellat.
chin   two (the distance of) fingers   in wonder

—O sigui, que és veritat que van existir!
Oh   is   -that- (it) is true that (they) did to exist
     So

—Sí —va dir el seu pare, animant-lo a
Yes   did say -the- his father encouraging him to

enfilar-se   a la bicicleta estàtica.
climb -himself- at the bicycle   static
                 on   stationary

El nen pedalava amb l'alegria d'un explorador que
The boy pedaled with the joy of an explorer that

tasta per primera vegada l'hospitalitat d'un planeta
tastes for (the) first time the hospitality of a planet

nou però, al cap d'una estona, el pare va
new but at the end -of- a while the father did
            after

manar-li que parés, si forçava el cos l'endemà
order him that (he) stop if (he) forced the body the next day

estaria   cruixit   i   la   mestra   de   l'escola   podria
(he) would be   grinded   and   the   teacher   of   the school   could
         wasted

sospitar   que   havia   comès   alguna   infracció.
suspect   that   (he) had   committed   some   infraction (of the law)

Al   cap   d'un   mes,   el   mòbil   va   informar-los
At the   end   -of- a   month   the   cellphone   did   inform them
   After

que   el   govern   enduria   la   llei.   Ara   també
that   the   government   was hardening   the   law   Now   also

   seria   delicte   caminar   massa   de   pressa.
(it) would be   (a) crime   to walk   too much   of   (a) hurry
                           in

   Tot   s'anava   orientant   cap   a   la   inactivitat,
Everything   -itself- was   orienting   end   to   the   inactivity
                  heading   towards

cap   a   la   manca   absoluta   d'esforç.   L'esforç   ja
end   to   the   lack   absolute   of effort   The effort   already
towards

el   feien   els   mòbils.   De   mica   en   mica,   l'ambient
it   did   the   cellphones   Of   little   in   little   the atmosphere
                        Little by little

es   va   tornar   insuportable   fins   que   un   dia   la
-itself-   did   become   unbearable   until   -that-   one   day   -the-

seva dona va perdre la feina de l'oficina perquè
their woman did lose the/her work of the office because

algú va denunciar-la per haver pujat les
someone did report her for having ascended the

escales en comptes d'agafar l'ascensor. Havia
stairs in stead of to catch/taking the elevator Had

arribat el moment de prendre la decisió.
arrived the moment of to take the decision

Fugirien, travessarien la frontera
(They) would flee (they) would cross the border

de manera clandestina i buscarien nous
of manner clandestine/clandestinely and (they) would seek new

horitzons, més lliures, més dinàmics. La travessia
horizons more free more dynamic The crossing

per planúries i vessants, per boscos i
through plains and slopes through forests and

corriols va ser llarga, penosa i, sobretot, lenta
trails went to be long painful and above all slow

perquè, acovardits per tants anys de repressió,
because frightened for so many years of repression

van fer-la tota caminant i encara a poc a
(they) went to do it all walking and still at little to by

poc per no aixecar cap sospita. Per fi, la
little for not to raise any suspicion For end the / Finally

frontera, amb dos cartells de benvinguda. El
border with two posters of welcome The

cartell més gran deia: «Entreu a Hongria, terra
poster more big said Enter -to- Hungaria land

d'acollida de tots els esportistes mundials
of welcome of all the athletes world wide

refugiats». El segon cartell, una mica més petit,
refugees The second poster a little more small

advertia: «L'ús del mòbil serà castigat amb la
warned The use of the cellphone will be punished with the / by

pena de mort». Animat pel seu pare,
punishment of death Animated by -the- his father / Encouraged

l'Ernest, dòcil, va llençar el mòbil al
-the- Ernest docile did throw away the phone to the
his

contenidor custodiat per la guàrdia fronterera.
container looked after by the guard (of the) border

La seva mare va imitar-lo i amb el seu pare
-The- his mom did imitate him and with -the- his father

van contemplar com el nen començava a
(they) did to contemplate how the boy started to

caminar de pressa, primer tentinejant el terreny,
walk of hurry first stumbling (over) the terrain

després cada vegada més decidit, corrent muntanya
after every time more decided running mountain

avall amb la mateixa felicitat pura i innocent
down with the same happiness pure and innocent

que li van veure reflectida a la cara el
that to him (they) did see reflected in the face the

dia que va aprendre a caminar.
day that (he) did learn to walk

Déu i el senyor Gratacòs

God and the Mr. Gratacòs (God and Mr. Gratacos)

Diuen	que	en	temps	remots,	abans	de	néixer
They say	that	in	times	remote	before	-of-	being born

els	nostres	avis,	a	l'edat	mitjana	o
-the-	our	grandparents	in	the age	middle	or

abans	i	tot,	succeïa	de	vegades	que	el	rei
before	and	all	it happened	of	times	that	the	king
even before					sometimes			

dubitatiu	i	perplex	d'un	reialme	incògnit	o
doubtful	and	perplexed	from a	kingdom	unknown	or

algun	estudiós	escèptic	que	vivia	envoltat	de
some	studious	skeptic	that	lived	surrounded	by

llibres	i	no	gosava	creure	en	res,	convocava
books	and	not	dared	to believe	in	nothing	convoked
						anything	

savis	de	les	diverses	religions	conegudes	i
wise men	from	the	different	religions	known	and

els demanava que disputessin entre ells
them asked that they discuss amongst them(selves)

per escatir quina era la fe veritable i el déu
to find out which was the faith true and the god

de debò. Si més no, això explicaven cròniques
of duty if more no that explain chronics
real at least

antigues, en les quals casualment sempre
old in -the- which coincidentally always

guanyava la disputa dels savis aquell que
won the argument of the wise men that one which

professava la mateixa creença que aquell qui,
professed the same belief as that one who

després de la disputa, n'escrivia la crònica. En
after -of- the argument wrote of it the chronicle in

qualsevol cas, aquesta pràctica de l'antigor
any which case that practice from -the- antiquity

va arribar a oïdes del senyor Gratacòs
did arrive to (the) ears of -the- Mr. Gratacòs
arrived

—Bonifaci Gratacòs—, que vivia de tota la vida en
Bonifaci Gratacòs who lived of all the life in
his entire life

una cantonada de la plaça de l'església d'un
a corner of the square of the church of a

barri de cases baixes construïdes
neighborhood of houses low built

als anys cinquanta per gent vinguda
in the years fifty by people (having) come
in the fifties

d'Andalusia a la ciutat, ni molt gran ni molt
from Andalusia to the city neither very big nor very

petita, on havia nascut el senyor Gratacòs,
small where had been born -the- Mr. Gratacòs

i on vivien ara persones de tots els colors,
and where lived now people of all -the- colors

indumentàries, llengües i religions.
dress languages and religions

Potser perquè se sentia ell mateix com un
Perhaps because -himself- felt he himself like an

44

antic rei o com un savi venerable, el
ancient king or like a wise man venerable -the-

senyor Gratacòs, que no creia en Déu, però que
Mr. Gratacòs who not believed in god but who

no hauria matat mai ni una mosca
not would have killed -n-ever not even a fly

perquè sí (només, només, si molt emprenyava) i
because yes only only if a lot it was bothering and
just because

s'hauria fos abans de pujar a
-himself- would have melted before -of- getting on ti

l'auto-bús sense bitllet, va voler fer com es feia
the bus without (a) ticket did want do like one did
wanted to

abans i preguntar a savis de totes les
before and ask -to- wise men from all the

religions quina era la seva manera d'honorar
religions which was -the- their way of honoring
what

els seus déus. Els segles havien passat i
-the- their gods The centuries had passed and

45

va trobar que el que s'esqueia no era que els
did find that that which happened not was that the
he found

savis de totes les religions es
wise men from all the religions -themselves-

discutissin per veure qui tenia la veritat. Com
discussed to see who had the truth as

deia un altre savi, poeta, el senyor Gratacòs
said an other wise man (a) poet -the- Mr. Gratacòs

tenia la intuïció difusa que el mirall de la
had the intuition diffuse that the mirror of -the-

veritat es va trencar tot d'una, potser en el
truth itself did break all of one perhaps in the
broke all at once

primer instant del món, i els trossos
first instant of the world and the pieces

van quedar tan escampats que gairebé tothom
did stay so spread out that almost everyone
ended up

en tenia un a ca seva. No era una cursa
of them had one at home his Not it was a race

per veure quin era el déu veritable. Era
to see who was the god true it was

més aviat saber com feia servir cadascú el tros
more soon to know how made serve each one the piece
rather each one made use of

del mirall de la veritat, el tros de rostre de
of the mirror of -the- truth the piece of face of

déu, que li havia tocat en sort o que havia
god that him had touched in luck or that he had
he had received by

estat capaç de trobar.
been able to find

Encara una altra diferència amb els reis i els
Yet an other difference with the kings and the
from

savis antics: el senyor Gratacòs, que no era
wise men ancient -the- Mr. Gratacòs who not was

rei i era molt discretament savi, no podia
king and was very discretely wise not could

convocar al rebedor de casa seva —un
convoke to the entrance hall of house his an

pis   petit   i   modest,   comprat
apartment   small   and   modest   bought

fa   molts anys   i   poc posat al dia–   els
it makes many years and little put to the day the
    many years ago   not very modern

ministres, sacerdots i   pastors de   totes les
ministers   priests   and pastors from all   the

religions, no hi haurien pas anat i menys
religions not there would have -not- gone and (even) less

tots   a la vegada, i   va decidir fer-ho
all   at the time   and he did decide to do it
     at once   he decided

a l'inrevés: seria ell qui aniria, humilment,
at the reverse   it would be him who would go humbly
the other way around

a veure'ls a   tots i cadascun   dels   qui
to see them -to- all and each of the ones who

fossin al seu abast a casa seva, els demanaria
was at his reach at house his them he would ask
   within his reach

d'assistir a alguna de les seves cerimònies, i
to attend -to- one of -the- their ceremonies and

hi	tindria	converses	tranquil·les,	al
there	he would have	conversations	calm	-at the-

voltant	potser	d'una	taula.	I,	així,	el	senyor
around	perhaps	-of- a	table	and	thus	-the-	Mr.

Gratacòs	va	començar	anant	a	la	rectoria	de
Gratacòs	did	start started		going	to	the	rectory	of

l'església	de	la	plaça	del	barri,	i	a
the church	of	the	square	of the	neighborhood	and	to

l'església	evangèlica	nova	que	havien	obert	a
the church	evangelical	new	that	they had	opened	at

l'avinguda,	i	a	una	altra	de	diferent	del
the avenue	and	to	an	other a different one	of	different	of the

barri	del	costat,	i	a	la	mesquita	de	la
neighborhood	of the	side next to (his)	and	to	the	mosque	of	the

plaça	de	més	amunt,	i	a	la	sinagoga	de	la
square	of	more	up further up ahead	and	to	the	synagogue	of	the

capital	a	poca	estona	de	tren.	I	quan
capital	at	little	while a little ways away	by	train	and	when

va haver fet les més evidents, les que
he did have done the most obvious ones the ones that
he had

sabia tothom, va fer mans i mànigues per
knows everyone he did do hands and sleeves to

trobar-ne de noves, en va trobar un munt,
find of them of new ones of them he did find a bunch
find new ones he found

algunes que ni sabia que existien, i
some of them which not even he knew that they existed and

per saber quines eren les seves cerimònies i
to know which were -the- their ceremonies and

les seves creences i, sobretot,
-the- their beliefs and especially

per damunt de tot, i això seria el nucli
for above of everything and that would be the core
above all

del mètode Gratacòs de coneixement de les
of the method Gratacòs of knowledge of the

religions, què havien fet els creients i els fidels
religions what had done the believers and the faithful

de cadascuna, a la vida i a la història, en
of each one in -the- life and in -the- history in

nom de la seva fe.
name of -the- his faith

D'aquell dia ençà, durant moltes setmanes, potser
From that day forward for many weeks maybe

mesos i tot, el senyor Gratacòs va visitar
months and all -the- Mr. Gratacòs did visit

temples grans i petits, sumptuosos i
temples big and small sumptuous and

misèrrims, cridaners o mig amagats, de la
very miserable that stuck out or half hidden from the

ciutat i de fora de la ciutat, i va parlar amb
city and from out of the city and did talk with

homes i dones, sacerdots i pastors, imams i
men and women priests and pastors imams and

rabins, monjos i monges, creients de totes les
rabbis monks and nuns believers of all -the-

creences. I va sentir càntics exòtics en
beliefs and he did hear canticles exotic in

llengües desconegudes, polifonies i instruments
languages unknown polyphonies and instruments

sonors, oracions cridades o pronunciades cap
sonorous prayers shouted or pronounced towards

endins com un mormol, cerimònies i litúrgies
inside like a murmur ceremonies and liturgies

amb vestimentes solemnes o amb roba de
with clothing solemn or with clothes of (the)

carrer, invocacions bellíssimes o estranyes a déus
street invocations very beautiful or strange to gods

del tot diferents o potser de vegades només una
of the all diferent or perhaps of times only a

mica diferents, com si fossin noms diversos d'un
little different as if they were names different of a

mateix déu. I va menjar plats exquisits fets
same god and he did eat dishes exquisite made

amb vegetals que venien de lluny o pans
with vegetables that came from far away or breads

consagrats o barreges que li costava d'empassar,
consecrated or mixtures that him cost to swallow down

vins i licors i aigües purificadores. I va
wines and liquors and waters purifying and he did

sentir narracions extraordinàries de com havia
hear narrations extraordinary about how had

estat creat el món i de com les divinitats
been created the world and about how the divinities

vetllaven o deixaven de vetllar pels
watched over or stopped -from- watching over -for- those

qui l'habitaven o sobre tot allò que per a
who inhabited it or about all that which

cadascú era sagrat i improfanable, com un
each one was sacred and inviolable like an

immens llibre de meravelles.
immense book of wonders

Però sobretot el senyor Gratacòs va conèixer,
But — above all — -the- — Mr. — Gratacòs — did learn about / learned about

perquè per això va preguntar, històries de
because — for — that / about — he did / he asked — ask — stories — of

persones. De gent que feia el que feia en nom
people — of — people — that — did — what — they did — in — name

del seu déu i de la seva fe. I li
of -the- — their — god — and — of — -the- — their — faith — and — to him

van explicar històries admirables d'homes i de
they did / they explained — explain — stories — admirable — of men — and — of

dones que visitaven malalts i guarien
women — that — visited — sick people — and — healed

ferits i donaven menges i vestits i
injured people — and — gave — tasty foods — and — clothing — and

begudes a aquells qui més ho necessitaven, i
drinks — to — those — who — most — it — needed — and

oferien en nom de déu la seva vida i la
offered — in — name — of — god — -the- — their — life — and — -the-

seva hisenda i la seva saviesa a aquells que
their fortune and -the- their knowledge to those who

els envoltaven, per així servir millor el seu
them surrounded in order to thus serve better -the- their

déu i la fe que hi tenien. I va conèixer
god and the faith that in it they had and he did know / he learned about

també històries terribles de gent que moria i
also stories terrible about people who died and

patia persecució perquè creia en allò que
suffered persecution because they believed in that which

creia. Però, és clar, patia persecució i
they believed but it is clear / of course they suffered persecution and

era odiada i exterminada i maleïda per altres
were hated and exterminated and cursed by other

persones que creien en altres coses. Uns morien
people who believed in other things some died

en nom d'un déu i altres mataven en nom d'un
in name of a god and others killed in name of a

déu. D'un altre. I els qui aquí mataven, allà
god of an other and the ones who here were killing there

eren matats. I els que avui exterminaven
were being killed and the ones that today exterminated

eren demà exterminats. I la sínia
were tomorrow exterminated and the ferris wheel

semblava que no parava mai de fer voltes
seemed that not it stopped never -from- making laps
like ever going in circles

i a estones semblava que s'accelerava, com si la
and at times it seemed that it accelerated as if the
like

sang empenyés la sang. Quan va acabar el
blood pushed the blood when he did finish -the-
he finished

seu pelegrinatge per temples i assemblees,
his pilgrimage through temples and assemblies

consagracions i oracions, converses i més
consecrations and prayers conversations and more

converses, el senyor Bonifaci Gratacòs es
conversations -the- Mr. Bonifaci Gratacòs himself

va trobar un dia al cafè del racó de la plaça
did find one day at the cafe of the corner of the square
  found

de la ciutat amb la seva amiga Magdalena
of the city with -the- his friend Magdalena

Burrull, que estava al dia de les seves anades
Burrull who was at the day of -the- his goings
  up to date with

i vingudes per entre els creients de totes les
and comings for among the believers of all the
  throughout

creences i coneixia el seu escepticisme inicial,
beliefs and knew -the- his scepticism initial

i li va fer la pregunta que
and to him did make the question that
  asked

el mateix Bonifaci sempre tenia present.
the same Bonifaci always had present (in mind)
  Bonifaci himself

—Comptat i debatut, després de tant parlar
Counted and debated after -of- so much talking
  all things considered

i de tant comparar, has trobat la religió
and -of- so much comparing have you found the religion

veritable?
true

—No la buscava pas.
Not it I was looking for at all

—Doncs diguem-ho d'una altra manera: has
Then let's say it -of- an other way have you
let's put it

trobat la religió que més ajudi la gent a fer
found the religion that most helps -the- people to do

el bé, que la vida dels altres sigui millor?
-the- good so that -the- life of (the) others is better

En Bonifaci Gratacòs va mig incorporar-se de la
— Bonifaci Gratacòs did half get himself up from the
got up halfway

cadira, satisfet, gairebé eufòric. Va prendre un
chair satisfied almost euphoric he did take a
he took

glopet de cafè amarg, com si necessités un
sip of coffee bitter as if he needed an

instant per pensar, però no el necessitava,
instant to think but not it he needed

s'ho   sabia de memòria.
-himself- it he knew by   memory

—Totes.   Totes ajuden. Aquí o allà, ara o abans.
All of them all of them   help   here or there now or before

En nom de tots els déus hi ha hagut gent
in name of all the gods there have had people
                               there have been

bona que ha fet coses admirables pels altres.
good that have done things admirable for -the- others

Com si creure en déu fes sortir allò de millor
as if believing in god made come out that of best
                            the best

que tenien dins. No   n'he   trobat cap que
that they had inside not of them I have found any which

no ho hagi fet mai. Totes les que conec, i
not it has done ever all the ones that I know and

sospito que probablement també les que
I suspect that probably also the ones that

desconec.
I don't know

El   senyor Gratacòs va tirar el cos enrere i
-The-   Mr.   Gratacòs did pull the body back   and
                                pulled   his

va fer un sospir, potser de cansament.
did make a   sigh   maybe from   tiredness
    sighed   due to

—Però...
  But

—Com ho saps   que   hi ha un però?
  How   do you know that there has a   but
                           is

—Perquè sospires...
  Because   you are sighing

—Doncs sí,   hi ha un però. Però en nom de
  Well   yes there has a   but   but   in name of
                  is

totes aquestes mateixes religions un dia o altre
all   these   same   religions one day or another

s'ha   matat algú,   s'ha   fet   una injustícia,
has been killed someone has been done   an   injustice
                        committed

s'ha   perseguit un innocent. Unes més i   altres
has been persecuted an innocent some more and others

menys. Unes sobretot en el passat, altres encara
less some above all in the past others still

avui. No hi ha déu que estigui lliure d'aquesta
today not there has (a) god who is free from this
is

pena: la d'haver vessat sang en el seu
punishment that of having spilled blood in -the- his

nom...
name

La Magdalena Burrull somreia: el coneixia molt
-The- Magdalena Burrull was smiling him she knew very

bé, el seu amic. Li sabia els topants.
well -the- her friend of him she knew the nooks and crannies
she knew him like the back of her hand

—Per tant, continues sense creure en res.
For so much you continue without believing in anything
therefore

—Certament, continuo sense creure en res.
Of course I continue without believing in anything

Perquè en nom de totes les religions s'ha fet
because in name of all the religions has been done

el   mal.
-the-   bad

El   silenci de   la   Magdalena tenia un punt de
The   silence of -the-   Magdalena had   a   tip of
was a bit

teatral, preparant l'embranzida final.
theatrical   preparing   the dash   final

—T'entenc   molt bé. Però només hi ha una
I understand you very well but   only   there has one
is

cosa que no em lliga. També en nom del   no
thing that not me join   also   in name of -the- not
adds up for me

creure en   res   s'ha   fet   el   mal.   S'ha
believing in anything has been done -the- bad one has

matat en nom de totes les religions, però   s'ha
killed   in name of all   the   religions   but   one has

matat també en nom d'estar en contra de totes
killed   also   in name of being -in- against -of- all

les religions. També   el   no creure està tacat de
the   religions   also   -the- not believing is   touched by

sang. Potser, de fet, aquesta taca la du
blood maybe of done this stain it takes
in fact

al damunt qualsevol paraula noble, qualsevol
to the front any word noble any
before

creença i qualsevol somni, amb déu o sense...
belief and any dream with god or without

A en Bonifaci Gratacòs li va costar molt
To — Bonifaci Gratacòs -for him- it did cost much
For it was very hard

dir el que havia de dir.
to say that which he had to say

—Doncs potser tens raó. Però jo prefereixo no
Well maybe you have reason but I prefer not
you're right

creure en res.
to believe in anything

—I tant! Però parlar amb els qui creuen t'ha
And so much but talking with those who believe you has
most certainly

fet més savi.
made more wise

63

—I més bo?
And more good

—Vés a saber.
Go to know
who knows?

La   Magdalena   va estar   a punt de   dir: doncs
-The-   Magdalena   did   be   at point of   say   well
                        was   about to

no se'n parli   més.   Però no ho   va dir.
not about it speak   (any) more   but   not   it   she did say
let's not speak about it   she said

Perquè   en   van parlar   més.
because   about it   they did speak   more
                        they spoke

Vegades i vegades. Potser encara   en   parlen
times and times   maybe   still   about it they speak
again and again

ara, al   cafè de la plaça de la ciutat, mentre
now in the cafe of the square of the city   while

senten tocar les campanes i,   una mica més
they hear sound the   bells   and   a little more

lluny, el crit a l'oració dels muetzins.
far the cry to -the- prayer of the Muezzins

Vuit setmanes i tres dies
Eight weeks and three days

Vuit	setmanes	i	tres	dies.	I	l'hivern	encara
Eight	weeks	and	three	days	and	the winter	still

aquí,	fent	espetegar	els	vidres	de	les	finestres.
here	making	crack	the	glass-es-	of	the	windows

Estic	cansada	del	fred	i	del	vent.
(I) am	tired	of the	cold	and	of the	wind

Faig	el	ronso	cada	matí	sota	l'edredó	i
(I) do	the	slacker	every	morning	under	the comforter	and
I lay around							

només	trec	el	nas	quan	s'escola	un
only	(I) take out	the	nose	when	-itself- filters	a
		my				

filet	de	sol	entre	les	escletxes	de	la
thin trickle	of	sun(light)	between	the	cracks	of	the

persiana.
blinds

Fa **exactament** **vuit** **diumenges** **que** **no** **vaig** **a**
It makes / exactly / eight / Sundays / that / not / (I) go / to
It has been / / / / since

dinar **a** **casa** **els** **pares.** **Encara** **no** **els**
have dinner / at / (the) house (of) / the / parents / Still / not / to them
/ / / my

ho **he** **dit.** **Ni** **això** **teu,** **ni**
it / (I) have / told / neither / that / of yours / nor
/ / / / / about you

això **de** **la** **feina.** **Els** **germans** **sí** **que** **ho** **saben.**
that / of / -the- / work / The / siblings / yes / that / it / know
/ about work / / / My / / do indeed

Em **cuiden** **de** **lluny.** **En** **Pau**
Me / (they) take care of / from / afar / -Me- / Pau

s'ha **donat** **d'alta** **a** **InfoJobs** **per**
himself has / given / of membership / to / InfoJobs / to
/ has subscribed

reenviar-me **cada** **dia** **les** **ofertes** **de** **feina**
forward me / every / day / the / offers / of / job
/ / / / / job offers

mentre **duri** **el** **meu** **atac** **de** **tecnofòbia** **(no**
for as long as / lasts / -the- / my / attack / of / technophobia / not

m'acosto **a** **Twitter** **ni** **a** **Facebook** **ni** **que**
-myself- (I) approach / to / Twitter / nor / to / Facebook / nor / that
/ / / / / / / not even if

em matin, no fos cas que ensopegués amb
me (they) kill not be it (the) case that (I) come across -with-
lest

el teu somriure o amb el teu "M'agrada" en
-the- your smiley face or -with- -the- your Me pleases in
"Like"

alguna foto d'un amic d'una amiga d'un amic d'un
some photo of a friend of a friend of a friend of a

cosí, i per descomptat no llegeixo el teu blog,
cousin and for discounted not I read -the- your blog
it goes without saying

i amb prou feines m'animo a obrir el
and with enough efforts (I) motivate myself to open the
with difficulty

correu electrònic de tant en tant). La Julieta
mail electronic from so much in so much -The- Julieta
from time to time

m'envia whatsapps matiners cada tres o
sends me WhatsApp messages (in the) morning every three or

quatre dies, per no atabalar-me (com em
four days in order to not overwhelm me as me

coneix...), i em diu "Bon dia, preciosa,
-she- knows and me says Good day precious
morning

com t'has llevat avui?" i hi adjunta
how yourself have (you) gotten up today and to it she adds
how are you doing

fotos del trosset de paisatge del Montsant que
photos of the little piece of landscape of the Montsant that

ha escollit aquell matí per a la seva
she has chosen that morning for -to- -the- her

sessió de ioga. L'Ester em truca sovint (ella
session of yoga -The- Ester me calls often she

sí, que per algun motiu és la germana
yes since for some reason she is the sister
does (call) there's a reason

gran), i li passa el telèfon al Nil o
big and -to him- she passes the phone to -the- Nil or

a la Berta perquè a mi
to -the- Berta so that -to- -me-

em caigui la bava de tieta i me'n vagi a
to me falls the saliva of auntie and -myself of it- (I) go to
as their aunt I drool over them

dormir amb un somriure. En Jan m'ha començat
sleep with a smile -The- Jan me has started

a   escriure   cartes   de   les   d'abans,   per
to   write   letters   of   the ones   from before   through
the kind

correu   postal,   des de   Bordeus,   per   animar-me,
mail   postal   from of   Bordeaux   for   to cheer me up
from

perquè   sap   que   m'agraden.   Em   diu   que
because   (she) knows   that   I like them   Me   (she) says   that

els   vagi   a   veure.   Que   en   Luc   em   farà
them   I (should) go   to   see   That   -the-   Luc   me   will make

col-i-flor   per   sopar   si   li   canto   la   cançó   d'Els
cauliflower   for   dinner   if   him   (I) sing   the   song   by The

Amics   de   les   Arts   (Ai   Jean-Luc,   ai   Jean-Luc...)
Friends   of   the   Arts   Ai   Jean-Luc   Ai   Jean-Luc

mentre   els   torno   a   recordar   que   estan
while   them   I return to   remind   that   (they) are
I remind them again

fets   l'un   per   l'altre.
made   the one   for   the other
made for each other

L'un   per   l'altre.   Com   tu   i   jo   fins
The one   for   the other   like   you   and   me   until
for each other

fa   dos mesos   i   tres dies.   L'una   per
it makes   two   months   and   three   days   The one (girl)   for
   two months ago

l'altra.   Era   tan   fàcil de   dir, d'escriure, de   pensar,
the other   It was   so   easy   to   say   to write   to   think

de   fer.   Tu,   la   mixeta   sense   nom   i   jo,   en
to   do   You   the   kitten   without   (a) name   and   me   in

aquest   pis   de lloguer   del   Poblenou   amb
this   apartment   of   rent   of -the-   village-new   with
       rented

terrasseta   i   vistes   al   mar. Tan   senzill   com
(a) small terrace   and   views   to the   sea   so   simple   as
            as

això.   Tan   difícil   com   això.   Què   vols
that   so   difficult   as   that   What   do you want
      as

que et digui,   en   el   fons   sempre   he   estat
that you (I) tell   in   the   background   always   (I) have   been
   me to tell you   deep down

feta   a   l'antiga.   A   mi   em   feia   feliç   la   vida   que
made   at   the old   To   me   -me-   made   happy   the   life   that
   old-fashioned

teníem,   amb   dissabtes   de   mercat,   diumenges   de
(we) had   with   Saturdays   of   market   Sundays   of

rambla i vermut, dimecres de cinema als
rambla and vermouth Wednesdays of movie theater in the boulevard

Verdi i vespres d'estiu sopant amb els amics a
Verdi and evenings of summer dinner with the friends at

la terrassa. Em feien feliç les tardes d'hivern de
the terrace Me made happy the afternoons of winter of

sofà i manta i sèries infinites, els matins de
sofa and blanket and series endless the mornings of tv

cap de setmana mandrejant entre els llençols, els
head of week lazing about between the bed sheets the end

dinars a casa dels meus pares, al pis del
lunches at house of the my parents to the apartment of the

Guinardó, o de la teva mare, a Premià. Això de
Guinardo or of -the- your mom to Premia That of

la criatura, no ho sé, potser només era una
the creature not it (I) know maybe only was an

idea, però és que tot quadrava tant,
idea but is that all framed checked out so much

saps, que ni em va passar pel cap
do you know (how) that nor me did pass through the head

que a tu no et fes il·lusió. Que no
that to you not you made illusion That not

t'imaginessis un menut o una menuda corrent
yourself you imagined a small or a tiny current

per la masia de Gualba, amb l'Ester i els
by the farmhouse of Gualba with -the- Ester and the

nebots i el fill de l'Albert les setmanes que
nephews and the son of -the- Albert the weeks that

li toca. Em cau bé, l'Albert. "Veus?", em
to him touch Me falls well -the- Albert (You) see me
                  pleases

diria ara la Julieta si em sentís, "que les coses
would say now the Julieta if me heard that the things

s'acabin no vol dir necessàriament que
themselves end up not wants to say necessarily that

hagin fracassat." També em diria que quan
(they) have failed Also me would say that when

una porta es tanca s'obren mil finestres,
a door itself closes itself open one thousand windows

"Mira l'Ester, quan es va divorciar semblava
Watch -the- Ester when herself did divorce (it) seemed

que s'hagués d'acabar el món i ja ho
that herself would be of to finish the world and already it

veus, ara, està contentíssima, i l'Albert és
(you) see now (she) is very happy and -the- Albert is

un tio genial..." Si la meva germana petita em
an uncle great If -the- my sister small me

sentís, em diria que la vida és canvi
heard me (she) would say that -the- life is change

continu, que el que resisteixes persisteix, que tot
continuous that it that (you) resist persists that all

ens passa per aprendre i evolucionar, i totes
us pass for to learn and evolve and all

aquestes frases de PowerPoint tan boniques de
these sentences of Powerpoint so beautiful of

dir i tan difícils d'aplicar quan les coses et
to say and so difficult of to apply when the things you

passen a tu.
(they) pass to you

M'agradaria, no et pensis, ser una mica
Me (it) would please not you think to be a little (one)

com la Julieta. Viure feliç en una casa okupa a
as the Julieta Live happy in a house occupied at
                                                 squatted

la muntanya amb vuit o deu persones, treballant
the mountain with eight or ten people working

en projectes autogestionats (que deu ser com
in projects self-managed that (it) must be like

estar a l'atur però sense angoixa i fent
to be to the unemployment but without anguish and do

el que t'agrada), llevar-te per meditar quan
it that you pleases take off yourself for to meditate when

surt el sol i després enviar una foto del
comes out the sun and after to send a photo of the

moment a la teva germana mitjana, que
moment to -the- your sister middle that

probablement no es llevarà fins d'aquí a dues
probably not it will take until from here to two

hores i que encara viu en el cercle de
hours and that still lives in the circle of

l'aferrament que és la causa de tot dolor. No, si
the attachment that is the cause of all pain No if

la teoria me la sé pel cap dels dits.
the theory to myself her (I) know for the tip of the fingers

Però no hi puc fer més: fa dos mesos
But not there (I) can make more (it) does two months
it has been

i tres dies que estic aferrada a tu, que no
and three days that (I) am clinging to you that not

se m'acut cap altra manera de viure més
themselves me (I) love any other manner of life more

bonica que la que teníem abans que s'acabés tot,
beautiful that her that (we) had before that itself ended all
than it

abans que jo decidís engegar-ho tot a pastar fang,
before that I decided to start it all to graze mud

per ser més exactes.
for to be more exact

El mòbil m'avisa que en Pau m'ha reenviat les
The phone me warns that -the- Pau me has forwarded the

ofertes de feina del dia. Sembla la propaganda
offers of work of the day (It) seems the propaganda

del súper, això. Sous a la baixa i hores a
of the super that Below to the low and hours to

l'alça (dues jornades per un sou). Clico a
the rise two days for a salary (I) click on

"Suprimeix" i les envio a la paperera. Potser
Delete and them send to the bin Maybe

la clau de tot és no imaginar-se cap vida, i
the key of all is not imagine oneself (the) end (of) life and

anar fent i prou.
go doing and enough

Em poso el xandall i baixo a comprar el
Me (I) put (on) the tracksuit and go down to buy the

pa. De tornada, a la bústia, trobo la carta
bread Of return at the mailbox (I) find the letter
When returning

d'en Jan. Es casa. Amb en Luc, esclar. A
of -the- Jan (He) is home With -the- Luc of course To

Catalunya, esclar (a França no és legal). Diu que
Catalonia of course to France not is legal Says that

vol que els canti la cançó de «Jean-Luc» a
(he) wants that they sing the song of «Jean-Luc» to

la cerimònia –Tens una veu preciosa, Laieta, t'hi
the ceremony You have a voice precious Laieta there

hauries de dedicar–. Em fa ràbia per què
(you) should of to dedicate Me (it) makes angry for what
so

m'han caigut les llàgrimes mentre llegia i
me (they) have fallen the tears while (I) read and

s'han esborrat unes quantes línies, i ja
themselves have erased some few lines and already

no hi ha manera de recuperar-les. Per sort
not there is manner of to recover them For luck
Fortunately

s'ha salvat la postdata: Bonica, quan rebis
has been saved the postdata Beautiful when (you) receive

aquesta carta envia'm un whatsapp, per saber que
this letter send me a whatsapp for to know that

ja podem avisar la resta de la família.
already (we) can warn the rest of the family

Té aquests detalls, en Jan. Sap que tinc
(He) has these details -the- Jan (He) knows that (I) have

una mica de complex de germana del mig, la
a little of complex of sister of the middle Her

que ningú no veu gaire, que hi és però no es
that no one not sees hardly that there is but not one

nota, que no és ni la gran ni la petita, ni
notes that not is neither the big nor the small nor

el gran ni el petit. Deu ser per això que no
the big nor the small (It) must be for that that not

m'he   preocupat   mai   de   fer   les   coses   gaire
myself have   worried   never   of   to do   the   things   barely

com   tocaven.   Total,   ni   se   m'exigia   ser   la
as   (they) touched   Total   nor   themselves   me asked   to be   the

més   responsable,   com   a   l'Ester   o   a   en   Pau,
more   responsible   like   to   -the- ester   or   to   -the-   Pau

ni   em   reien   les   gràcies   com   a   en   Jan   i
nor   me   (they) laughed   the   graces   as   to   -the-   Jan   and
         they smiled at

a   la   Julieta.   Ni   tan   sols   em   van   parar   gaire
to   the   Julieta   Nor   so   only   me   did   to stop   very long

atenció   quan   vaig   aparèixer   a   casa   amb   la
attention   when   (I) did   appear   at   house   with   -the-

Mariona,   amb   disset   anyets   acabats   de   fer.   En
Mariona   with   seventeen   years   finished   of   to make   In
                                      just

canvi,   aquest   tema   amb   en   Jan   els   va   costar
change   this   topic   with   -the-   Jan   them   goes   to cost

molt   més.   Tot   deu   ser   qüestió   d'expectatives,   i
much   more   All   (it) must   be   question   of expectations   and

sembla clar que els pares no se n'havien
(it) seems clear that the parents not themselves they had

fet cap ni una, pel que fa a mi. No
done any nor one for it that does to me Not
concerns

s'han mostrat mai ni gaire entusiasmats
themselves have shown ever neither hardly enthusiastic

ni gaire desesperats amb el que feia. M'he
nor hardly desperate with it that (I) did Me (I) have

guanyat fama de maldestra, despistada i
won fame of (being) spoiled clueless and

entranyable. Aquests darrers anys, l'únic que
hearty These last years the only (thing) that

m'havia sortit bé eres tu. I ja ho
myself (I) had to come out well are you And already it

veus.
(you) see

Torno a la Julieta i als seus ensenyaments
(I) return to -the- Julieta and in -the- her lessons

-que les coses s'acabin no vol dir que
that the things themselves end up not wants to say that

hagin fracassat-, i me la imagino a la
have it failed and to myself her (I) imagine at the

muntanya amb la seva gran família de gent
mountain with -the- their big family of people

diversa que també es lleva ben d'hora ben d'hora
diverse that also itself takes well of hour well of hour
an hour an hour

per fer ioga i que organitza tallers de cuina
for to do yoga and that organize workshops of kitchen
to

vegana i de flors de Bach, i penso que
vegan and of flowers of Bach and (I) think that

m'aniria bé passar una temporada amb ells.
me (it) would go well to pass a season with them

Vés a saber, potser m'agrada i tot, això
(You) go to know maybe me (it) pleases and all that
I like it

del tofu i dels mantres i dels paisatges a
of the tofu and of the mantras and of the landscapes to

l'hora que surt el sol. En tot cas, alguna cosa
the hour that comes out the sun In all case some thing
the time   any

he de fer, no puc passar-me unes altres vuit
(I) have of to do not (I) can pass me some other eight

setmanes i tres dies en aquest estat de letargia
weeks and three days in this state of lethargy

mig depressiva i descaradament autocompassiva,
half depressed and shamelessly self-pompous

oi?
right

Oi. Obro les finestres perquè entri aire fresc,
Ok (I) open the windows for that to enter air cool

acabo la dutxa amb un bon raig d'aigua freda,
(I) finish the shower with a good spurt of water cold

substitueixo el xandall pels texans nous i un
(I) replace the tracksuit by the jeans new and a

jersei de color verd viu (per si és cert allò de
jersey of color green live(ly) for if (it) is certain that of

l'esperança)   i   m'assec   a   taula   amb   la   porta   de
the hope   and (I) sit down   to   table   with   the   door   of

la   terrassa   també   oberta,   l'ordinador   al   davant
the   terrace   also   open   the computer   to the   front

i   un   esmorzar   com   Déu   mana.   Obro   el
and   a   breakfast   as   God   commands   (I) open   the

correu   electrònic   i   començo   a   dir-t'ho   tot.
mail   electronic   and   (I) start   to   to tell you (I) have   all

Que   no   volia   espantar-te.   Que   amb   fill   o   sense,
That   not   wanted   to scare you   That   with   son   or   without

vull   tenir-te   a   prop.   Que   no   cal   ni
(I) want   to have you   at   near   That   not   is necessary   neither

que   visquem   juntes,   que   podem   fer   allò   del
that   (we) live   together   that   (we) can   make   that   of the

"living   apart   together",   el   'cadascuna   a   ca   seva'
living   apart   together   the   each one   at   home   theirs

de   tota   la   vida.   Que   t'estimo,   bonica.   I   que
of   all   the   life   That   you (I) love   beautiful   And   that

demà   mateix,   a primera hora,   baixaré
tomorrow   same   at (the) first   hour   (I) will go down
              on the very day

fins a la platja a meditar com m'agrades   i
until to the beach to meditate as   me pleases and

t'enviaré   una foto preciosa   per   Whatsapp,
you (I) will send   a   photo   precious   through   whatsapp

perquè somriguis com somric jo quan me les
because   (you) smile   as   smile   I   when   me them

envia la Julieta.
sends the   Julieta

www.ingramcontent.com/pod-product-compliance
Lightning Source LLC
LaVergne TN
LVHW011214080426
835508LV00007B/774